Very Writing

AGE 3-5

Sue Barraclough
Educational consultant: Margaret Deehan
Illustrated by Derek Matthews

This workbook is designed for younger children as an introduction to writing. It will help them to begin learning the skills and concepts that form the basis of literacy. These include:

· understanding the relationship between the spoken and the written word
· knowing the difference between drawing and writing
· realising that each letter has its own shape and sound
· improving hand to eye co-ordination and pencil control
  to develop the ability to write clearly and fluently

How to help your child

· Keep sessions short (about 15-20 minutes) and regular.
· The exercises are meant to be enjoyable as well as educational, so always stop if your child is
  not relaxed or has lost concentration.
· Go through each page to make sure your child understands what to do.
· When you read the instructions with your child, run your finger along the sentence from left to right,
  so children become used to the movement of reading and writing.
· Use at least four different coloured soft pencils or felt-tip pens when doing the exercises, so that
  your child can follow the instructions and enjoy the colouring.
· Use the correct sound for each letter (as shown on page 2), rather than its name.
· Offer plenty of praise and encouragement for the smallest efforts. The exercises are simple but
  they are a challenge to a young child.

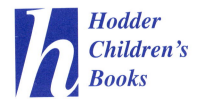

Hodder
Children's
Books

**The only
home learning
programme
supported by
the NCPTA**

Shapes and sounds

These are the letters we are going to learn. Look at the first letter **a** and its picture clue. **a** has the sound at the beginning of **a**pple. Try saying the sounds of some of the other letters using their picture clues.

Help your child by emphasising the correct sound for each letter. Say the sound of the letter carefully for your child to copy – 'duh', not 'dee', 'suh', not 'ess' etc.

Balls of wool

 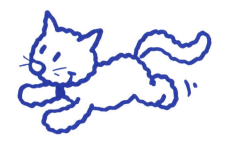

The three little kittens have been playing with coloured balls of wool. Choose a colour for each kitten, and show how each ball of wool has unwound all the over page.

What a tangle!

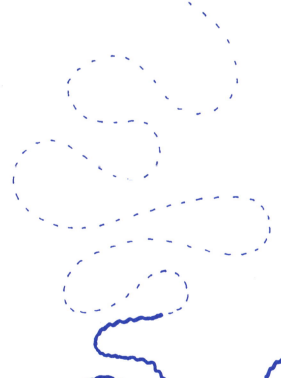  

Scribble shapes

Choose a colour for each crayon and use that
colour to fill each shape with scribbles.

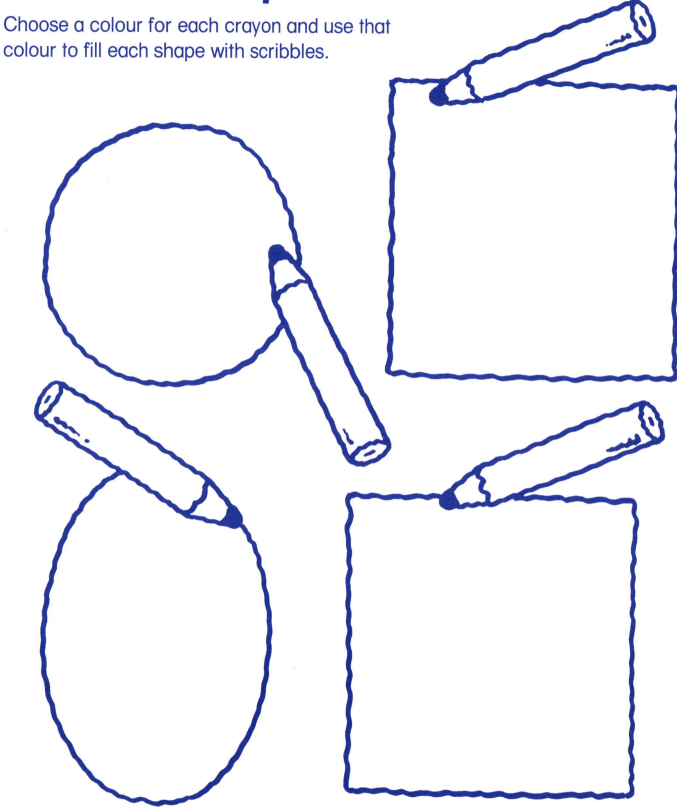

Scribble patterns

Look at the first pattern. It's a zig-zag line. Go over the line with
your finger. Then draw a zig-zag across the page with your pencil.

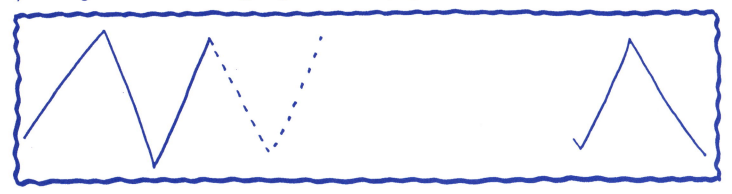

Here are two more patterns to finish.

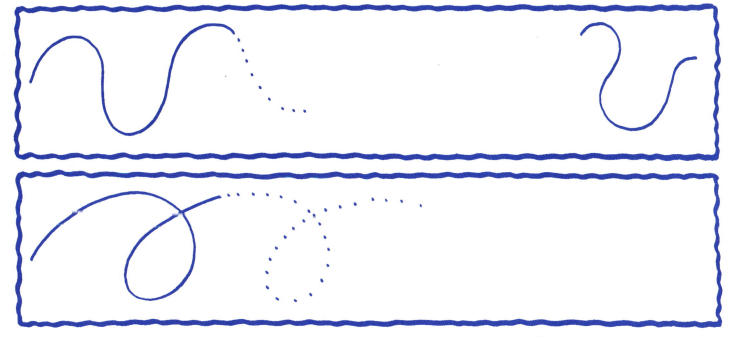

Now draw your own pattern across the page.

Toy shop colouring

Colour all the toys in the shop window.

Provide children with a variety of pens, pencils and crayons so they can choose those that feel most comfortable.

Animal paths

The bee is buzzing from flower to flower.
Let's draw its path in a bright colour.

Draw the frog's path as it hops from lily pad to lily pad.

The duck swims around the lily pads to her ducklings.

Here children are following instructions and drawing particular patterns which will help with forming letter shapes later on.

Steering clear

Fly the helicopter across the city. Draw its
path – make sure you don't bump into
any tower blocks!

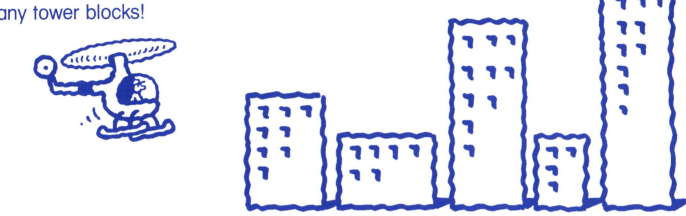

Steer the boat in and out of the islands.

Fly the spaceship in
and out of the planets
and back to earth.

Encourage children to think of their pencil as steering around the buildings, islands
and planets. It is important that exercises like this are fun and make sense to children.

Fairy tale journeys

Snow White is lost in the forest. Follow her
path to find the dwarfs with your finger first.
Then draw her path with a blue pen.

Draw a red line to show the prince's path through
the thorns to reach Sleeping Beauty in the castle.

Prince Charming is looking for Cinderella.
He must hurry past the Ugly sisters
and then pick up the glass slipper.

Draw his path with a green pen.

Don't worry if your child can't keep the pencil on the path, it's all good practice in pencil control.

Snail trails

Snails leave a trail behind them as they slide along.
Draw a squiggly trail behind each snail.
Start at the dot ●.

Colouring

Colour the insects and flowers in brilliant colours.

Just picking up and putting down the pens while colouring is an important part of learning to hold the pen for writing.

Pony races

Pretend you are riding the pony. Draw your path
over the jumps as you race across the page.

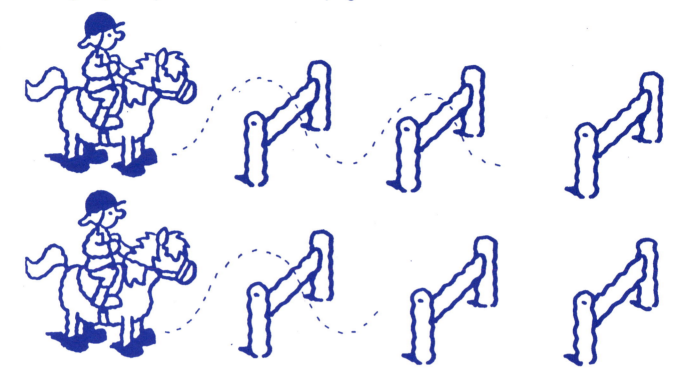

Now draw your path in and out of the stripy poles.

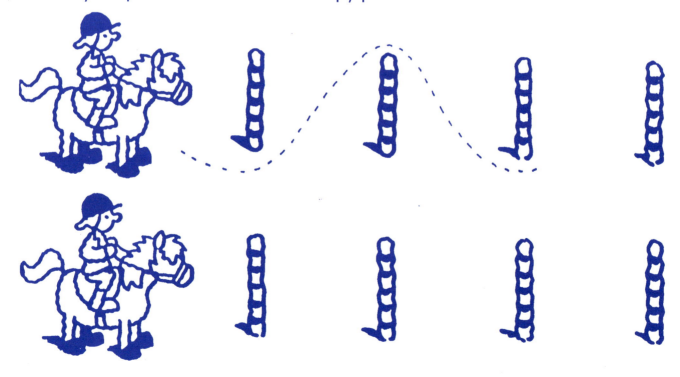

Odd one out

Can you spot the odd one out in each row?
When you have found it, colour the odd shape red.

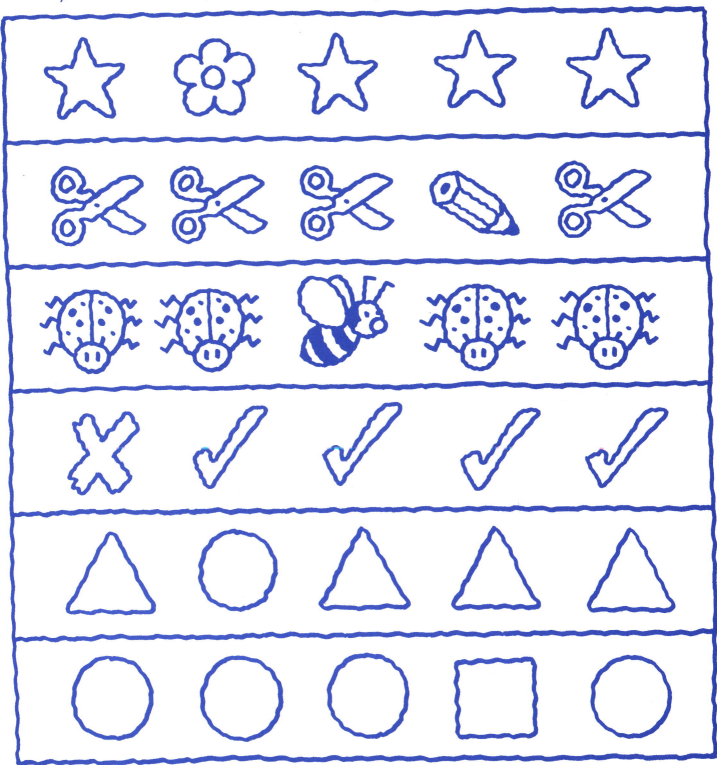

Butterflies

Look at the spotty butterfly. Can you see another one that looks the same? Draw a line to join them, then match up the other butterfly pairs.

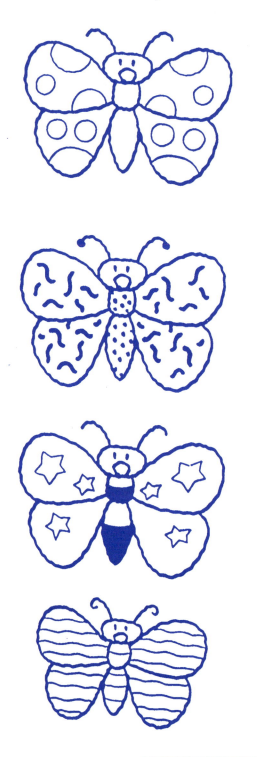

Children are asked to match by looking at the patterns, which will help with letter recognition. Encourage your child to colour the butterflies.

Match up

There is a balloon. Can you see another one? Join the
balloons with a line. Then match up the other pairs.

Round the track

Look at the direction each vehicle is facing. Then draw
its path all the way around the track.

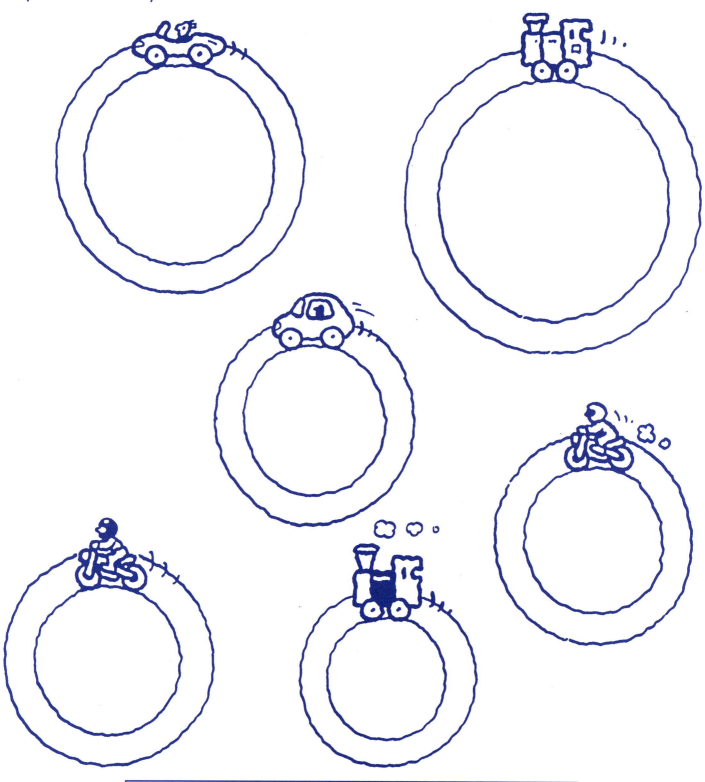

This exercise gives children the chance to practise an anti-clockwise circle which
will give them confidence when they tackle writing letters o, a, g and d next.

Letter o

Finish these funny faces by drawing a circle.
Start at the dot ● and follow the arrow ←.

The octopus has caught a letter **o**!
Can you spot any other letter **o**'s?
Colour them orange.

Practise writing letter **o**. Start at the dot ●
and follow the arrow ←.

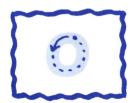   

Children often find a circle the easiest shape to form, which is a good start for writing letter o. Finding a letter amongst other shapes improves letter recognition.

Letter a

These snakes are making letter **a** shapes.
Practise letter **a** by drawing along each
snake from its head to the tip of its tail.

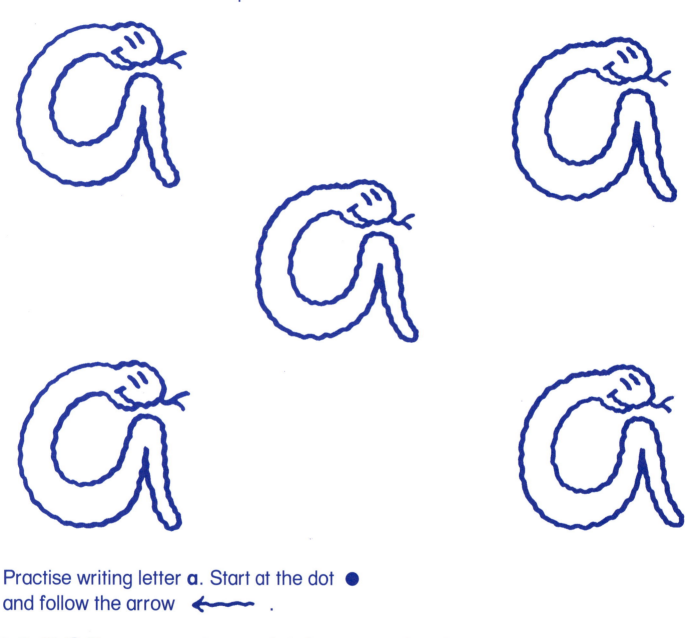

Practise writing letter **a**. Start at the dot ●
and follow the arrow ←——— .

Most letters are a combination of curved and straight lines, and forming
them in one flowing movement can be difficult for a young child.

Letter d

Practise writing letter **d**. Start at the dot ●
and follow the arrow ←⌇ .

The **d**uck is looking for her
ducklings. She must follow
the letter **d** path to find them.
Colour the letter **d**s to show
her which way to go.

Letter g

Can you find a **g**orilla, a **g**oat and a **g**irl hiding in this picture? When you've spotted them, colour them **g**reen.

Practise writing letter **g**. Start at the dot ● and follow the arrow ← .

Your child will gradually learn that each letter has a different shape and sound.

Letter match

Let's find a latter **a**. When you have spotted it
colour it **blue**. Then find another **a** and colour it to match.
Now match and colour the other letter pairs.

Write a word!

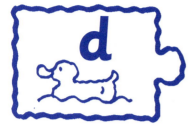  

Let's use some of the letters you have written to make a word. Go over the letters with your finger, then write over them with your pencil.

Colour the dog show picture.

Writing

AGE 3-5

Sue Barraclough
Educational consultant: Margaret Deehan
Illustrated by Lorna Kent

This workbook is designed to help your child learn the following important writing skills and concepts:

- confidence in drawing patterns - vital for developing pencil control and continuity of movement
- hand-eye coordination
- understanding the difference between drawing and writing
- familiarity with the 26 letter shapes
- understanding that each letter shape has its own sound
- becoming accustomed to reading and writing from left to right.

How to help your child

- Keep sessions short (no more than 20 minutes) and regular.
- The exercises are intended to be enjoyable as well as educational. It is important that your child sees that learning is fun, so always stop if they are not relaxed or have lost concentration.
- Build confidence. Offer praise and encouragement for the smallest efforts. The exercises are very simple but they are a real challenge for a young child. It is important that these basic skills are acquired thoroughly.
- Have at least four different coloured pens or pencils (preferably felt-tip pens or soft pencils) to do the exercises. Your child will be able to see clearly what they have achieved, and picking up and putting down the different pens is good practice in itself. Give your child plenty of room to practise – left-over wallpaper is ideal.
- Talk your child through more complicated letters as they write them. Page 2 gives a guide to how each letter should be written. In the workbook the letters are grouped according to their starting points and similarities in shape and formation.
- Always use lower case letters, not capitals.

Hodder Children's Books

The only home learning programme supported by the NCPTA

All the letters

This page shows how to form each letter. It is important that you describe each letter correctly for your child. Say the sound of each letter, rather than its name in the alphabet - 'duh' and not 'dee' for letter d, 'fuh' and not 'eff' for letter f, etc.

Scribble picture

Start from each paint tube using the right colour. Draw a line with each colour, making swirls, squiggles and zigzags.

First, help your child to colour each paint tube correctly. Scribbling is a very important stage in learning to write. Don't let your child worry about forming shapes, simply encourage them to keep the pencil on the paper all the time and fill as much space as possible with a continuous line and an even pressure. The pencil should be held by the thumb and first finger, resting on the middle finger.

Animal paths

Draw each animal's path across the page. Remember each animal has a
different pattern.

Fairground patterns

Make cones for these ice-creams.

Draw sticks for the toffee apples.

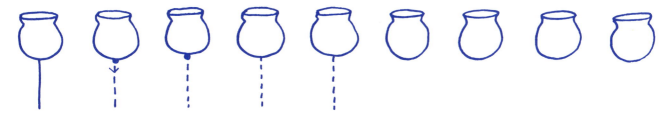

Draw a big cloud of candy floss on each stick.

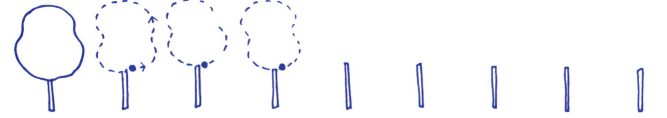

Draw over the cones and fill each empty cone with sweets.

Draw a lollipop on each stick.

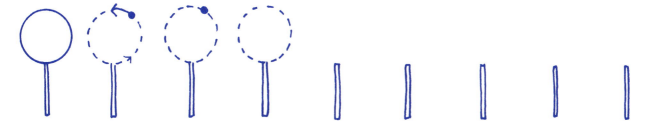

Snow scene

The artist needs your help to finish the picture. Use bright colours.

Encourage your child to notice shapes and patterns around them, at home and outside.

Which way to school?

It's time to go to school. Follow each child's path, using a different coloured pen for each one. Keep your pen on the path all the way.

a, c and o

apple

cake

orange

Draw circles to finish these pictures. Start at the dot • and follow the arrow ↗.

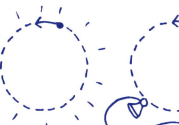     

Draw wheels on the cars.

  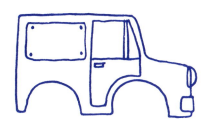

Practise writing **a**, **c** and **o**.

     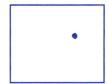

     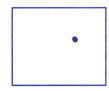

   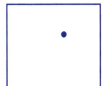 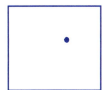 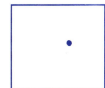

d, g and q

Read these names slowly, listening to the sound of the first letters.

duck    **goat**   **queen**

Practise writing **d**, **g** and **q**.

What are the first letters? Write **d**, **q** or **g** in the box.

These letters all have the same starting point as a, c and o. Children need to build on what they have already learned, trying to write the letters in one continuous movement.

r, m and n

robot

monster

nose

Draw in the lamp posts

Draw over the arches in the bridge.

Draw over the sea monster's shape.

Now try writing **r**, **m** and **n**.

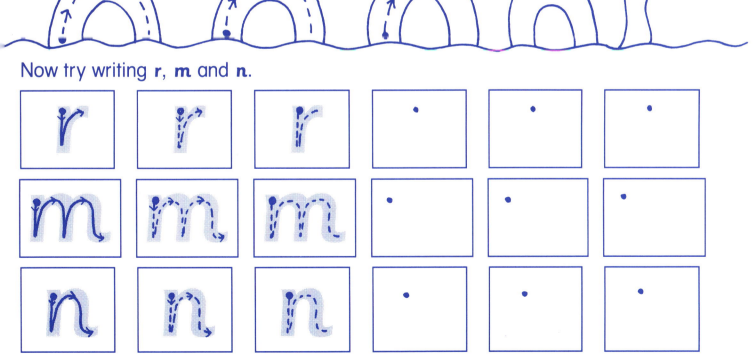

These letters share the same starting point and have a similar formation.

h, b and p

hammer **balloon**  **parrot**

Draw round each bubble. Follow the arrow.

Draw the humps for the camel.

Finish drawing the perches for the parrots.

Now try writing **h**, **b** and **p**.

  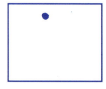 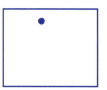 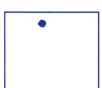

    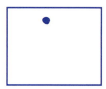 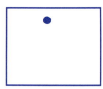

These letters are difficult for children because they are a combination of straight and curved lines. As with d, q and g, encourage them to write them in one movement.

i, j and l

ink

juggler

lamb

Draw over the dotted lines to finish the tails and trunks on these elephants.

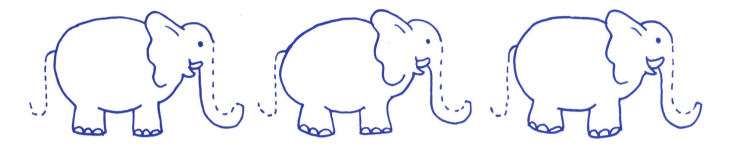

Make this snake stripy.

Now practise writing **i**, **j** and **l**.

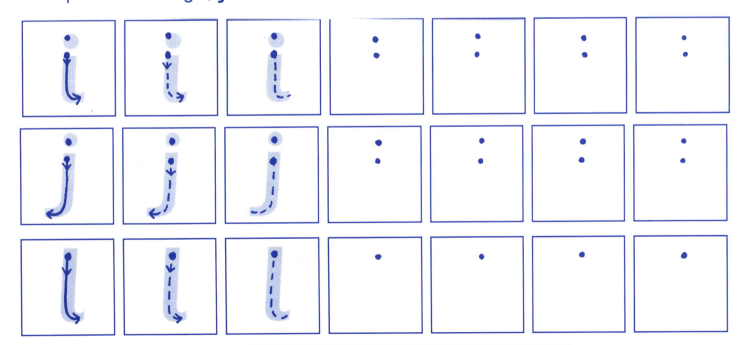

Your child has now begun to write fifteen letters - over half the alphabet!

u and y

umbrella

yo-yo

Draw big smiles on these faces.

Now try writing **u** and **y**.

Look at this picture. Can you see a child **yawning** and a child **yelling**? Find a child **upside-down**, a child **under** something and a child climbing **up**! Now draw a ring round each letter **u** and each letter **y** on this page.

Learning to distinguish and formulate 26 letters takes time, so it is important that pre-writing exercises are entertaining. Help your child listen out for words beginning with u and y, and see if they can find any others in the picture (e.g. yo-yo, umbrella).

e and s

elbow

sock

Practise writing **e** and **s**.

   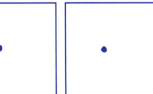

    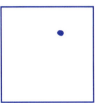 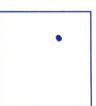 

Say the name of each picture. If it begins with **e**, colour the picture red. If it begins with **s**, colour the picture blue.

f, k and t

feather   **kite**   **teapot**

Practise writing **f**, **k** and **t**.

Look at each picture and say its name. Listen to the first letter, and write **f**, **k** or **t** in the box.

This is quite difficult, and younger children may need help.

v, w, x and z

van windmill x as in fox zebra

Draw in the crocodile's teeth.

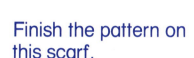

Finish the pattern on this scarf.

Finish the tractor's trail.

Practise writing **v**, **w**, *x* and **z**.

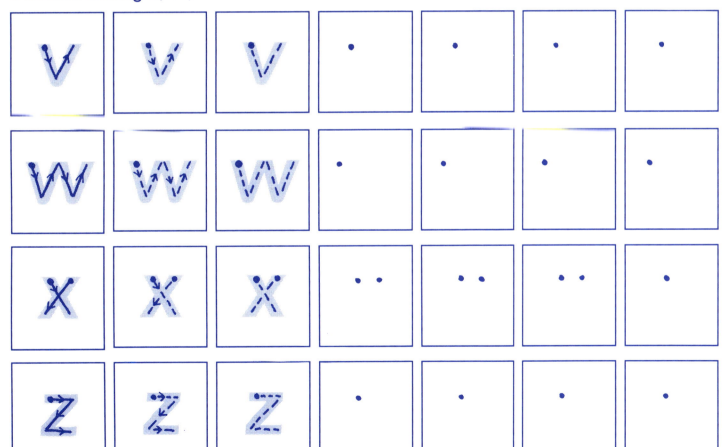

At school, your child will spend plenty of time getting to know each letter, so there's no need to hurry.

Initial letters

Look at all these pictures. They all have names beside them, but the first letters are missing. Listen to the sound of the letter, then write it in.

___ **oat**

___ **adder**

___ **amera**

___ **ouse**

___ **inosaur**

___ **eacock**

___ **ountain**

___ **ocket**

___ **elicopter**

___ **andcastle**

___ **igsaw**

___ **elephone**

a e i o u

Say the words and listen carefully to their sounds.

apple   egg   igloo   octopus   umbrella

Look at the big letter at the beginning of the row and say the sound. Then look along the row. Can you see a word that starts with the same letter? When you find it, colour the picture.

a	hammer	glasses	arrow
e	cat	rabbit	elephant
i	mug	ink	teapot
o	apple	orange	pear
u	umbrella	flower	sun

Finish the words

Look at each picture and say its name. Then finish the words.

Write **a** or **e**.

t__p　　　**p__n**　　　**c__t**　　　**h__n**

Write **i** or **o**.

b__b　　　**d__g**　　　**p__n**　　　**c__t**

Write **u** or **a**.

c__p　　　**v__n**　　　**s__n**　　　**m__t**

Choose **a**, **e**, **i**, **o** or **u** to finish these words.

j__m p i n g

s k__p p i n g

h__p p i n g

Animal homes

It is just about to rain, so the animals are rushing home. Follow the paths with your pencil to find out where each animal lives. Then write the name of each animal under its home.

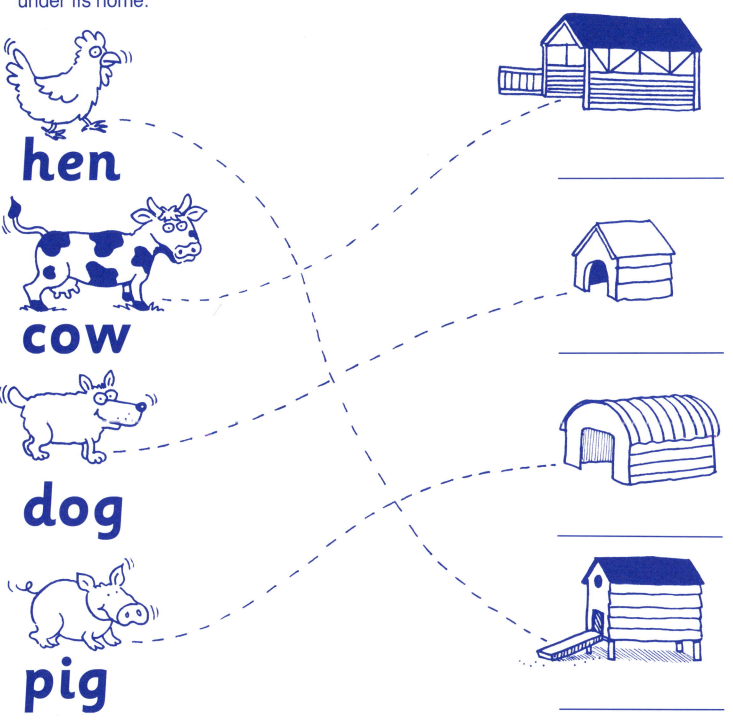

hen

cow

dog

pig

What is this?

Which word goes where? Finish the labels on the photographs using the words below.

bee   panda   sock   fish

Opposites

Here are some opposites.

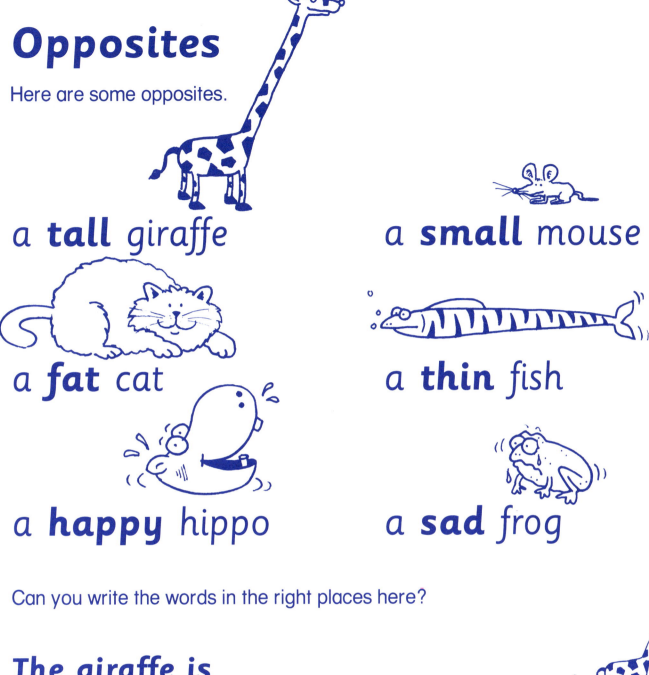

a **tall** giraffe

a **small** mouse

a **fat** cat

a **thin** fish

a **happy** hippo

a **sad** frog

Can you write the words in the right places here?

The giraffe is _____ .

The cat is _____ .

The hippo is _____ .

First crossword

Look at the big picture clues. Can you write the words? If you are not sure how to spell each word, look at the small picture clues in the boxes. The first letters of these names give you the right letter for each box.

Writing
Practice

AGE 3-5

Sue Barraclough
Educational consultant: Margaret Deehan
Illustrated by Emma Holt

This workbook provides pre-writing and writing practice for young children. It should help your child:

- improve pencil control and boost confidence with pre-writing patterns and mazes
- improve hand – eye coordination
- understand the difference between drawing and writing
- become familiar with the 26 letter shapes
- understand that each letter shape has a sound
- become accustomed to reading and writing from left to right.

How to help your child
- Keep sessions short (about 20 minutes) and regular.
- The exercises are intended to be enjoyable as well as educational so always stop if your child is not relaxed or has lost concentration.
- Build confidence. Offer praise and encouragement for the smallest efforts. The exercises are simple but they are a challenge for a young child. It is important that they master basic skills thoroughly.
- Have at least four different coloured pencils or pens (preferably soft pencils or felt-tip pens) to do the exercises. Children will be able to see clearly what they have achieved and picking up and putting down pens is good practice. Give children plenty of room to practise – left-over wallpaper is ideal.
- Talk children through more complicated letters as they write them. The pages dealing with specific letters show how each letter should be formed. The letters are grouped according to starting points and similarities in shape and formation.
- Always use lower case letters, not capitals.
- Whenever possible encourage older children not to copy letters when they write them. Instead they should look carefully at the letter, say its sound, cover the letter, write it and then check if it is correct. This will be a useful skill when they are learning to spell later on.

Hodder Children's Books

The only home learning programme supported by the NCPTA

Paint trails

Draw a coloured trail from the paint blob to the paint brush.

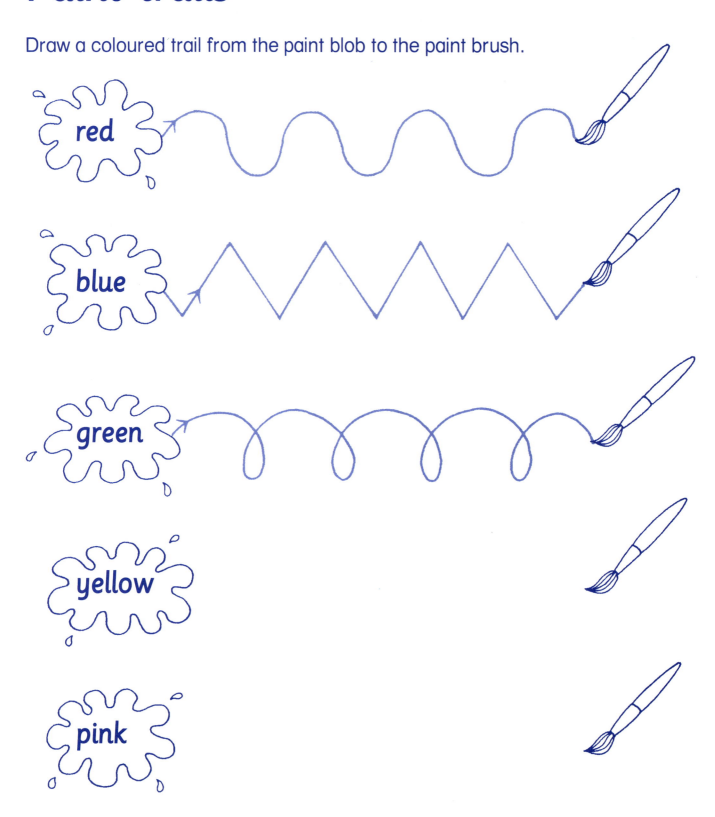

Same shape

Look at the first shape in each row, then make the other shapes match.

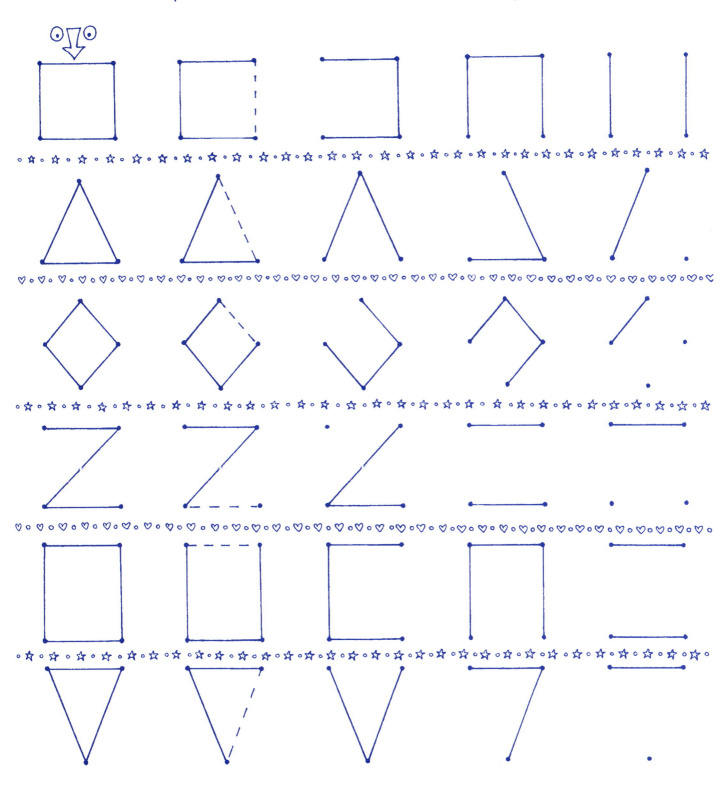

All the way home

Hansel and Gretel are lost in the woods. Use a blue pen
to follow Hansel's trail of stones to find their way home.

Use a red pen to draw Red Riding Hood's path through the woods.
Can you spot the Big Bad Wolf?

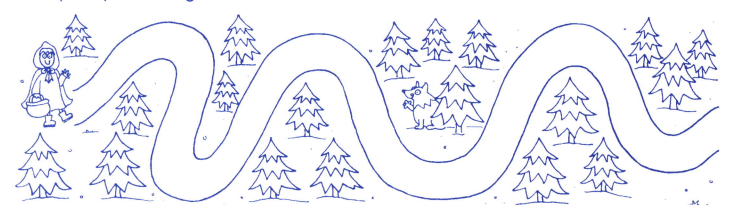

Goldilocks is running away from the three bears!
Can you show her the way home? Use a green pen this time.

Young children often find following paths difficult, so don't worry if they don't follow them exactly.

a, c, and o

Look carefully at each letter. Then draw a line to show which tower each block belongs to. Colour all the blocks in each tower the same colour.

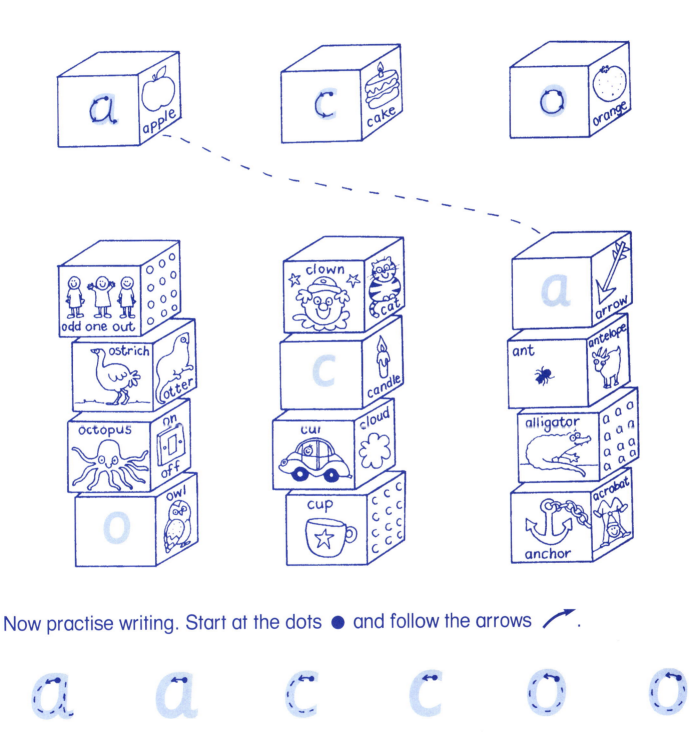

Now practise writing. Start at the dots ● and follow the arrows ╱.

Penguin paths

The penguins are playing in the ice and snow.
Draw over the penguins' paths.

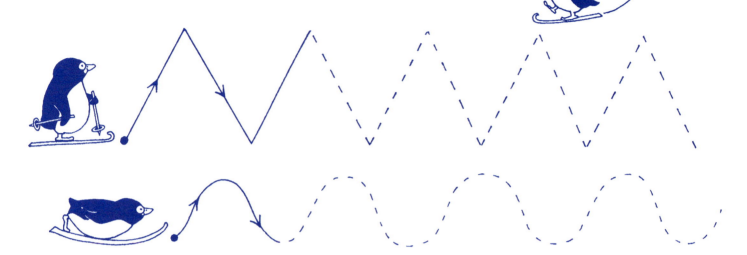

Draw each penguin's path right around the pond.

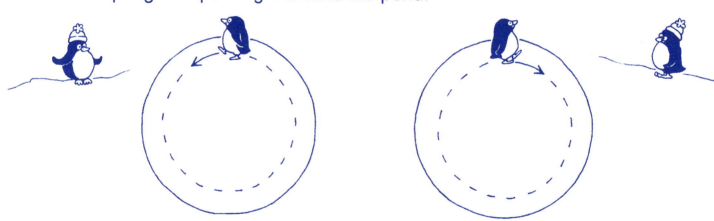

Draw a path going in and out of the icy igloos.

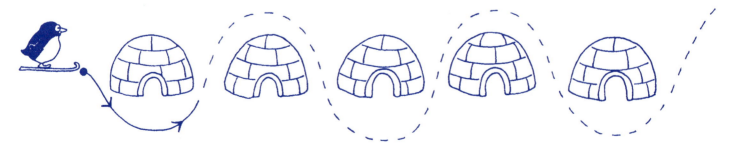

d, g and q

  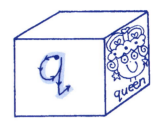

Draw along each path from the dot ● to the cross ✖.
Keep your pen on the page all the way.
Use a different colour for each path.

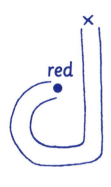
red

blue

orange

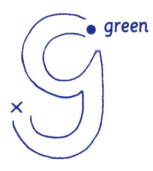
green

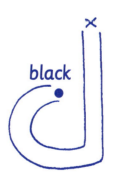
black

yellow

Now practise writing. Start at the dots ● and follow the arrows ➚.

These letters are similar in formation to a,c and o, but they are a mixture of straight and curved lines which children need to learn to write in one flowing movement.

Patchwork patterns

Colour in the patterns on each patch.
Use lots of different colours.

b, h, and p

Look carefully at each letter. Then draw a line to show which tower each block belongs to. Colour all the blocks in each tower the same colour.

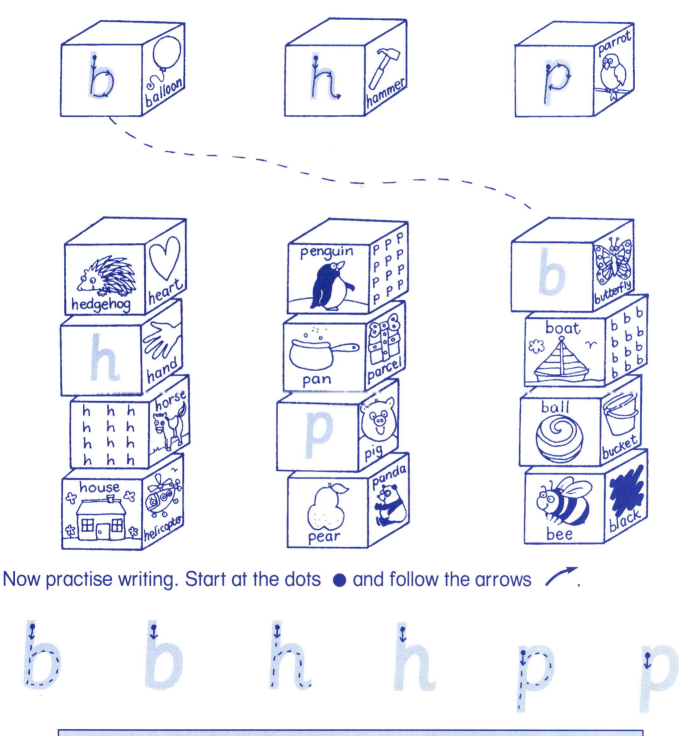

Now practise writing. Start at the dots ● and follow the arrows ↗.

b b h h p p

Around and about

The rocket is zooming around the world.
Draw its path.

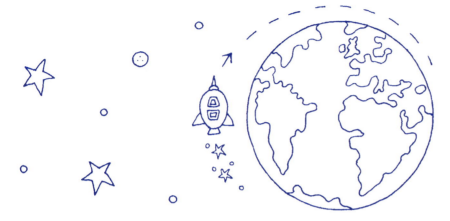

Draw the mouse's path
up the stairs.

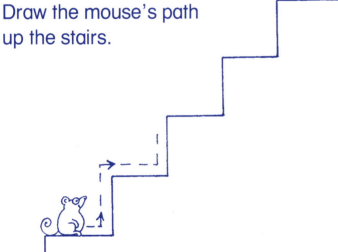

Draw steps
on the ladder.

Draw a path in and out of the bluebells.

In these exercises children are following instructions, which is an important skill,
and drawing particular patterns which will help with forming letter shapes later on.

r, m, and n

 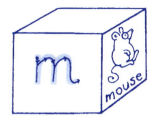 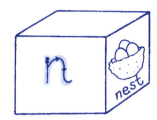

Draw frog hops across the page.

Now draw rabbit hops. Make these hops higher.

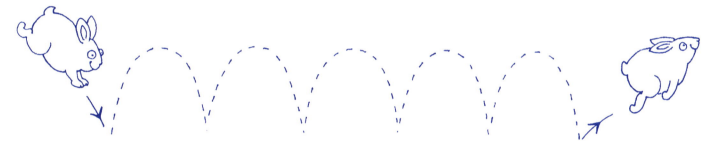

Make the lamb's hops even higher – boing! boing!

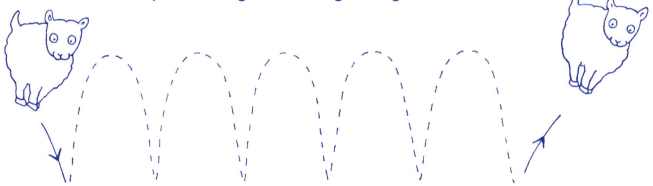

Now practise writing. Start at the dots ● and follow the arrows ⟋.

 r r m m n n

The pre-writing exercises are designed to give children confidence in drawing particular shapes and patterns. Writing letters then becomes less daunting.

Hugs and kisses

Did you know an X means a kiss and an O means a hug?
Pretend this is a birthday card from you. Write your name
and then fill the rest of the card with hugs and kisses.

Happy Birthday

Hugs and Kisses
Love from

e and s

Look carefully at each letter. Then draw a line to show which tower each block belongs to. Colour all the blocks in each tower the same colour.

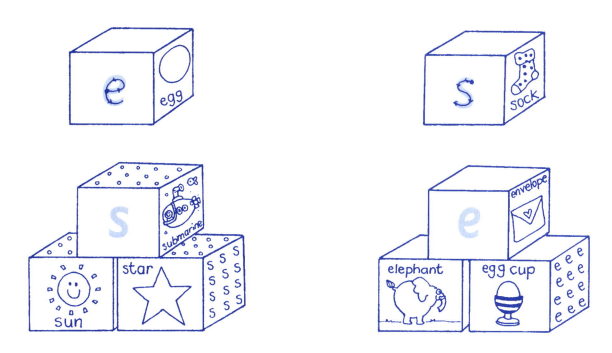

These snakes are making e and s shapes!
Colour the e snakes red and the s snakes blue.

Now practise writing. Start at the dots ● and follow the arrows ↗.

Patterns

Look carefully at each row. Can you finish each pattern?

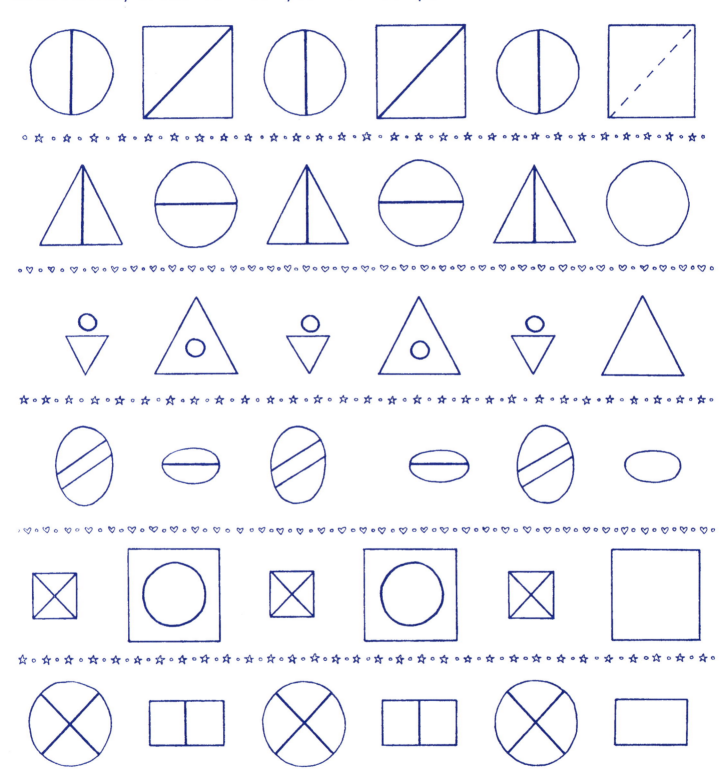

Children will need to look very carefully at each row. They might need help to start with, but they should be able to complete the exercise on their own.

i, j and l

 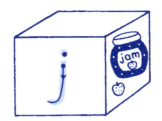 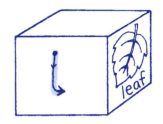

Draw stems for the flowers. Then colour the flowers red.

Draw trunks for the trees. Then colour the leaves green.

Now practise writing. Start at the dots ● and follow the arrows ↗.

i   i   i   j   j   l   l

f, k and t

Look carefully at each letter. Then draw a line to show which tower each block belongs to. Colour all the blocks in each tower the same colour.

 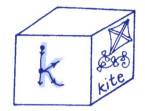 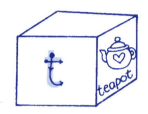

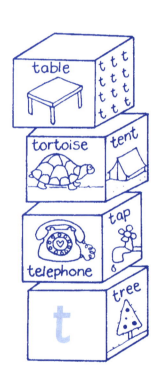 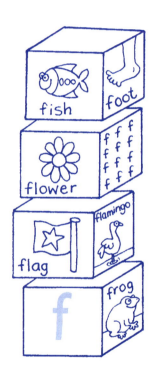 

Now practice writing. Start at the dots ● and follow the arrows ⟋.

Letter boxes

Look at the things in each box. Their names begin with the same letter.
Write this letter in the small box.

u and y

Draw over the dotted lines to finish the roundabout picture.
Then colour it brightly.

Now practise writing. Start at the dots ● and follow the arrows ↗.

Fancy dress

The children are dressed as their favourite animals.
Write an animal name on each box, then colour the costumes.

pig   bat   cat   hen

v, w, x and z

Look at each letter carefully. Then draw a line to show
where each block belongs and colour the blocks to match.

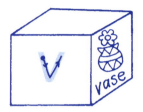  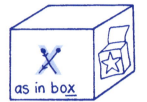 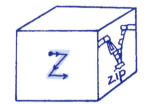

 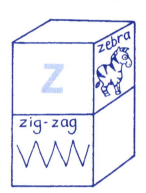 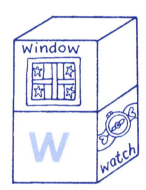 

Decorate one banner with zig-zags and one with crosses.

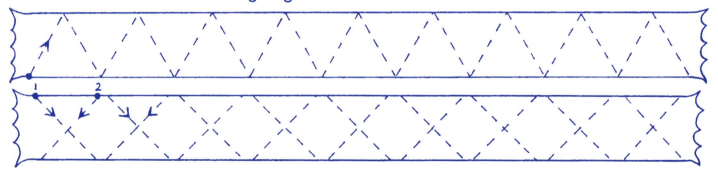

Now practise writing. Start at the dots ● and follow the arrows ⬈.

a, e, i, o, u

Say each word and listen to the sound of the first letter.

apple egg igloo orange umbrella

Look at the picture and say each word carefully.
Draw lines to join the words that rhyme.
Then write the missing letters.

h e n

d i g

h o p

j u g

f a n

p__g

p__n

v__n

m__p

m__g

Vowels are useful letters for children to learn. This exercise concentrates on the
rhyme, but make sure that children notice that the words share the same vowel.

Crazy golf

Can you find your way around the crazy golf alphabet course?
Draw the route around the course with a red pen,
using the alphabet at the bottom of the page to help you.

a b c d e f g h i j k l m

finish

n o p q r s t u v w x y z

Rhyme time

hole   house   box   hat

Use the picture clues to find out which word to write
to finish each of the rhymes.

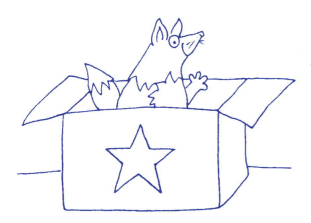

I am a fox
and I live in a _____.

I am a mouse
and I live in a _____.

I am a cat
and I live in a _____.

I am a mole
and I live in a _____.